Book 1
Fortran Crash Course

By: PG WIZARD BOOKS

&

Book 2
Hacking

By: PG WIZARD BOOKS

&

Book 3
Android Crash Course

By: PG WIZARD BOOKS

Book 1

Fortran Crash Course

By: PG WIZARD BOOKS

Step By Step Guide To Mastering Fortran Programming!

Fortran Crash Course: Step By Step Guide To Mastering Fortran Programming!

Table of Contents

Introduction

Introduction

Many beginners to coding worry that they are not going to be able to learn how to work with a new coding language. They feel that it is going to be too difficult to learn the language and that they will either not be able to do some of the programming that they want or that they just won't understand what is being said in the information. But when it comes to working with Fortran, you will find that learning how to code is a simple process.

In this guidebook, we are going to start out by talking about some of the information that comes with Fortran. We will also work on the first code for this language and discuss all the different parts that are going to be found inside of your code. This is a simple introduction to help you get some practice with writing your own code and ensures that you are able to get into some of the more complex situations that we will discuss later on.

Once we have these basics down, we are going to move on to some of the other things that you are able to do when it comes to working on your code in Fortran. We will take a look at writing some of your own loop statements, what strings and arrays are, working with conditional statements, and so much more. Even as a beginner, you will be able to use these options in order to make a really strong code and program as you want it.

When you are ready to get into coding and want to make sure that you are designing something that is strong and will work the way that you want, Fortran is one of the best coding languages to help you learn how to get it done. Make sure to use this guidebook to help you to get the basics to work with Fortran for all your coding needs.

Chapter 1: Learning the Basics of Fortran

As a beginner, you may have times that you are worried that a new coding language will be too hard for you to learn. You want to make your own programs, learn how to work in different operating systems, or have another goal that you would like to accomplish, but you worry that it is going to be too much work for you to accomplish because it will be too hard to do. But when it comes to learning how to work with Fortran (which is basically a contraction of Formula Translation), you are working with a great language that is designed for beginners, even for those that have no experience in coding before.

Fortran is considered one of the oldest programming languages that you can use and this can be a benefit as well as an issue. It is beneficial because you will be able to find this language anywhere that you want to look and the compiler, as well as the other add-ons, are all going to be free. It is a coding language that many scientists and engineers like to use because of all the functions that are built in and the fact that it is easily used with mathematical constructs. There are also many other things that you are able to do with this coding language, and since it is one of the oldest options around, you are sure to find lots of help and answers to ensure that you get the project done right.

What will I need to get started?

When you are ready to get started with Fortran, you will need to bring out a new text editor. There are several of these that are available, and you can choose the one that works for you. You need this because it allows you to out the codes so that the compiler, which you will need next, will be able to read out what you are doing and tell the computer how to behave. You are not able to use a word processor for this because these kinds of applications are not going to save files in plain text, which is required to make the compiler do its job.

Next on the list is the compiler. There are many options out there and most of them are going to be free as well so you can download these and not have to worry about adding in costs. Basically the compiler is going to take the words that you have written in the text editor and then change them around into something that the computer is actually able to read. You will just need to save your code and then the compiler will be able to execute it.

Some people find that working with an Integrated Development Environment, or IDE, is a great way to help make this a lot easier. This IDE is going to work similar to the text editor and the compiler in one so it saves you some time, especially when it comes to troubleshooting the written code. For those who are working on Windows computers, the IDE is really a good idea because it has an interface that is easy to sue and similar to what you are used to seeing on the Windows computer.

As mentioned, you could just use the text editor and the compiler, but the IDE does make it a bit easier to write your code. These combine both of the other two products in one and it is able to understand syntaxes of the code easily. In fact, it is going to be able to catch some of the errors that come up in the code as you are typing, saving a lot of time and accidents in the process.

The benefits of using Fortran for your coding

There are so many reasons why you may want to consider using Fortran as your coding language of choice. Whether you are looking to use it on the side as another coding language to master or this is one of the first coding languages that you are going to work with, the benefits of choosing this one are amazing. Some of the reasons that you would want to work with the Fortran coding language include:

- Easy to use: Fortran was designed for the beginner to learn how to use it. It is a simple language to work with and after looking at some of the codes in this book, you are sure to see that it is easy enough to learn how to work with.
- Has been around for a long time: Fortran is one of the first coding languages that came available for coders to use in their homes. This is a good thing because it is simplistic and easy to use. We are going to work on a few different codes inside of this guidebook and you will find that most of them are pretty straight forward and easy to write, even if you are a beginner. While some people feel that the fact that Fortran has been around for so long is a bad thing, it can mean so many good things for helping you to get the very best when working in coding.

7

- Great for the scientific community: this is a language that anyone is able to use for their own needs, but it is specifically important when it comes to the scientific community. If you have an occupation that is in this field, you will find that it is a good idea to learn how to use the Fortran code.
- Lots of programs still use it: even though this is an older coding language that you can use, there are still a lot of programs that use it. This means that you will have plenty of chances to use this programming language and to get some more practice.
- Can be modified for other languages: Fortran is one of the earliest coding languages that is out there so it has had many adaptations over the years. This means that there are versions that you are able to use and combine with some of your other programming languages. This makes it easier to do some of the more powerful things that you want to do with your coding.
- It is free: all the stuff that you need for Fortran, from the software itself to the IDE that you want to use with it, is all free to use. This makes it easier for everyone to use this language because you won't have to worry about all the costs that are associated with it.
- Has a big community: when it comes to using a brand new language, you want to make sure that you have a community that is able to answer your questions and make sure that you going on the right track. Since Fortran has been around for so long, there are many people who know how to use this and can be there to help you out.

There are many benefits to using the Fortran coding language. While some people prefer to go with another option that is easier or newer to use, there are still many people who want to work with Fortran because it is one of the first. It is a simplistic language to learn how to use even as a beginner, and it is able to get a lot of the coding and programming done that you would like. If you are looking for a coding language that is pretty easy to work with and is meant for beginners, you won't go wrong when choosing Fortran.

How to test my first code

Fortran Crash Course: Step By Step Guide To Mastering Fortran
Programming!

Now that we have spent some time talking about the things that you need to get started with the Fortran coding, it is time to test out one of our first codes. Once you have taken the time to install the IDE that you would like to use, it is time to double click on the icon so that the programming environment is going to open up. You can then create a brand new file but keep in mind that you may need to select on a Fortran file when you do this, just in case the IDE that you picked is able to read more than one language. So you will need to give it the extension of .f95 rather than of .txt so that you are able to compile these statements a bit later on.

One thing to keep in mind is that there are some other extensions that you are able to use when it comes to Fortran including .FOR, .F, and FPP. These extensions are going to tell the compiler was standards you are following with the work you do so make sure that you pick the one that you want and stick with it. You can experiment a bit to figure out which one you want to use.

So once you are done picking out the extension that you would like to use (we are going to stick with the .f95 one for now), we are going to need to type out the following code to get started:

program mytest

!this is a test

Print *, 'This is an output test'

end program mytest

After we have taken the time to type out this bit of code, it is time to execute it inside of the IDE. Your compiler will then go through and double check the parts of the code, looking to see if you have made any errors in the code before trying to run it. If there are any errors that show up, the IDE will let you know and ask you to fix it. If there aren't any troubles with the code, the compiler is going to generate and then execute the file. Basically, with this one you are going to find that the words "This is an output test" will show up on the screen if you typed it in the right way.

Breaking down this code

Now that we have taken some time to write our own code, it is time to break it down to make a bit more sense. Like a lot of the other coding languages that are out there, the Fortran language is going to take care of the different lines of the code, which are called statements, and then decide what it is going to do with each of them. So in the first line, the program is going to state the name of the program that you are trying to work with.

Then moving on to the second line, you are working with a comment. This basically means that you are writing a little note for yourself or for the other programmers that are taking a look at the code. The compiler knows that it shouldn't execute the comment since this is just a little note. You can add in as many comments as you would like inside of the code to describe what the different parts are going to do.

The third line of the code is the output command that is going to tell the compiler what it is supposed to display on the screen. It is going to show up in a single quote. You can make this statement as long or short as you would like, just make sure that you are using the right options with it. And then in the last line, the statement is terminating, or ending, the program that you just write.

Now, this is a pretty basic option that we are working on and only has four lines. There are many options that you are able to do with Fortran that will use more lines to get it done depending on the things that you are doing inside the code. There are also a few versions of Fortran that will have the code look a bit different. Basically all of them need to have the four same parts including the program name, the output statements (you may have more than one of these in some cases), end of program, and comments if you need them.

Making sure that you have all the right parts in place in order to write the code is important to helping the compiler to work with you on creating the code. And while there are many different data types that you are able to use, as we will discuss as we go on in this guidebook, they can be as simple or as difficult as you need to make the code work.

Chapter 2: Working on Loops in Fortran

When you are working on writing your own code inside of Fortran, you need to understand how to work with loops. There are many different times when you will want the code to keep repeating something, or do a specific action more than once. With the most basic form of your code, you would need to write this part of the code over and over again. Now, if you just want the code to repeat a few times, this may not seem like such a big deal, but what happens when you want to write out the code 100 times? Rewriting the same part 100 times can get tiring and old pretty quickly.

But with loops, you are able to tell the compiler to repeat the same steps until the conditions are no longer true. This could be five times and it could be 1000 times, but you would just need to write out a few lines of code to make this happen. Rather than having to write out the same instructions over and over again, you are able to set up the loop to do the same functions over and over again.

There are several different components that are going to be found inside of a loop to make sure that it is going to work. The main components include:

- Step: this component is going to tell the compiler that the procedure will need to be repeated at least once.
- Start: this is going to tell the compiler that it is at the beginning of your loop.
- Stop: this is going to tell the compiler that it is at the end of your loop.
- Var: this is a variable. It is in charge of telling the compiler how many times that you would need to have your code repeated.

How do these loops work?

Loops are going to begin when you set the start and then you define the var. they will explore what concept you are working with inside the var and decide when the conditions have no longer been met so this will all start. As soon as your statement is executed once, the amount to the var is going to go up by one so that you don't end up in an endless loop. So, if you want to make a table that goes from one to ten, the var would start at one and

then each time it goes up by one until it reaches ten. Let's take a look at a
sample code that shows how the loop function is going to work:

```
program loop_factorial

implicit none


    !definition of variables

    Integer::xfact=1

    Integer::x


    !computations of factorials

    Do x=1, 15

        Xfact=xfact*1

        Write*, x, xfact

    End do

End program loop_factorial
```

This one is a bit longer than what we are used to with the other code we
wrote, but it does show how the loop is going to work for you. This one is
going to make sure that the variable will keep going up by one each time
that you work with it, helping to keep things organized and to ensure that
you don't end up in an endless loop. If you do end up with a loop that
doesn't have a stop point, you are going to get stuck inside of the code and
have trouble getting out without closing the whole program.

There are a few different types of loops that you are able to work with.
Some are going to check the conditions of the statement before
determining whether or not to run the loop. If the conditions are not true
from the beginning, you are not going to get the loop to run at all and it is
going to head on to the next part of the code. This is known as the for loop.
And then the do while loop is going to run the loop at least one time, and
then run check the options to see if it meets the condition. The choice can
be the same, but it does depend on whether you want the code to run one
time or it doesn't matter.

The loop is one of the best things that you can work with when trying to make your code look nice and organized when on Fortran. You will be able to tell the loop how many times you would like it to run through the program, just using a few lines rather than rewriting the code all of the time. This is an efficient way to work inside of your code and ensures that the code is still able to work properly.

Chapter 3: Working with Strings and Arrays

When you are working with Fortran, you will find that strings and arrays are great ways to help keep the code organized. There are certain ways that you will be able to work with these in order to get them to execute inside of the code properly. In this chapter, we are going to spend some time talking about what strings and arrays are and how you would be able to work with them inside your code.

What are strings?

Inside of the Fortran code, all characters are going to be seen as one of two elements. They are seen as either single characters or contiguous strings. So what is the difference between them? With a contiguous string, you will notice that their length for syntax declaration is going to be passed, they will allow you to do notations on the substring, they won't allow you to do notation on arrays, they can contain descriptors if needed, and in some cases there are going to be hidden arguments inside.

When you want to declare a string inside of Fortran, you are going to use rules that are similar to declaring some of the other variables. So in order to do this, you would use the following option (we are giving the string an assignment of 10):

specifier :: variable_name

character(len=10)::name

Now in addition to working on the string, you will be able to work on substrings, which are basically just smaller parts of the string. They are going to be any part of the program that is executed and you are able to extract them if you wish. For example, if you have a long string that is several sentences long, you could work on a substring and just take out a few of the words to make it easier to read if you want. Here is an example of how you would be able to take out substrings from the string inside the code:

```
program string_concatenation

implicit non


        character (len=5) :: name

        character (len=50) :: announcement

        character (len=50) :: message


        name = 'Dana Caulfield'

        announcement = 'This is'

        message = 'I would like to give you a warm welcome to Prescott
Academy!'


print *, announcement, name

print * , message

end program string_concatenation
```

With this option you are going to get the message "This is Dana Caulfield. I would like to give you a warm welcome to Prescott Academy!" You are able to choose how much of the message you would like to do and you can keep it all on one line or on more than one. For example, you could choose to just have "This is Dana Caulfield" show up on the screen if you would like. This gives you some options to have a longer phrase there if you would like while also keeping it so that you get smaller patches as well.

Concatenation

Another thing that we are going to take a look at when working inside of Fortran is known as concatenation. You are going to notice that it will use the (//) symbol in order to show that this is inside the code. The concatenation property is the one that describes which programs are able to link back to each other. Because of these connections that are established, the main goal is to either draw attention over to another branch in the program, or to make sure that the framework is solid. In some cases the links are going to be for two separate programs, but often the subjects are going to be single elements.

You can also work with a process that is known as trimming. This is when you want to cut out parts of the line that are not necessary so that you get the right result to show up. Since there can often be elements inside the program that aren't needed and are known as trailing blanks, the process of trimming is going to help to get rid of some of this clutter so that you are able to just use the portions that are needed. It also helps your compiler to be able to read through the code faster.

There are a lot of things that you are able to do with the strings inside of your projects and you will be able to mess around with them a bit to get the strings to work out the way that you want. But using concatenation and trimming will help to ensure that you are using the strings in the proper manner.

Arrays

Arrays are another important part of working on your code. They are going to be in charge of storing information, such as variables and characters, that are similar. If the piles of data aren't stored in the proper way, it is going to be really hard for the computer to be able to interpret them. However, when you use the arrays properly to put this information in the right places, the compiler is going to have a better chance at running the program and the functions will be executed in the proper way. Some of the things that you should remember about arrays to make it easier include:

- If you would like to specify the individual elements, you are going to need to address them using the subscripts. The first element is going to have the subscript of 1.
- If you see the term "extent' it is going to describe the elements that are along a dimension. Keep in mind that this is a numerical value.
- On the other hand, if you see the term rank, it is going to describe the dimensions that they have, using a numerical value as well.
- When you see the term "size" this is going to describe the elements that the array has, using numerical values again.
- The shape of the array is going to consist of elements.
- They are going to be declared with the attribute of dimension.

- They are going to be linked to memory locations that are contiguous.

There are two types of arrays that you are able to find inside of the Fortran language. The one-dimensional arrays are the ones that will serve as vectors while the two-dimensional arrays are the ones that will serve as the matrices.

Now that we know a little bit more about arrays, it is time to understand how you are going to be able to declare the arrays. Luckily this is a process that is pretty easy to complete. The rule is to specify the dimension that you desire, and then the compiler will be able to take a look at the elements that are involved and determine if they are an integer or real. For example, if you want to declare an array that is the Caulfield Lair and you want to give it seven elements, you would use the following code to make it happen:

real, dimension (7) :: Caulfield Lair.

Now you can also choose to declare an array that is two dimensional. Let's say that we are still using the example of Caulfield Lair from above, but we are going to make it so that the elements are 7 by 7. To do this, we are going to use the following syntax:

integer, dimension (7, 7) :: Caulfield Lair.

If you would like to make sure that you are assigning the right values to your arrays, you will find that the process is pretty simple. You just need to work on the array and then enter in the amount that you would like to use. You do have some choices when it comes to doing this because you can either do it on a single element that you want to change or you can work it out on the whole array. Let's take a look at an example of how this would work. Let's say that we want to add in the value of 3 to all of the elements would need the following code:

do I = 1, 7

  Caulfield Lair = i*3.0

end program do.

But on the other hand, if you would like to assign the value of 3 to just the first level of the array and then add different numbers to the other levels, you would need to use the following code to make it happen:

Caulfield Lair (1) = 3

Working with strings and arrays are a good way to make sure that you are getting the code to work in the right way. The strings are going to be statements that happen inside the code and make it easier for you to write out the different things that you would like to have happen, either by adding in the whole string to the code or just having a few parts as you see fit. The arrays are going to be responsible for holding large pieces of data in a way that is easier to look through and reach inside the code. Both of these are going to be important to ensuring that you get more out of the code and that   it   works   the   way   that   you   want.

Chapter 4: Manipulating the Variable Amounts

Now at this point we are going to take some time to look at the different operators and variables that you are able to use inside of your code. So far at this point we have learned a bit about how to create a simple program. But there is a lot of manipulation that you are can do inside the code and operators are a great way to help you to do this. The operators inside of Fortran is going to be a great way to do mathematical functions while also getting these results to show up on the screen. With all that we have learned so far about this program, it is now possible to work on a short program on our own that will help to manipulate the amounts of variables. So basically inside of this chapter, we are going to learn how to make our program in Fortran do some basic math.

First we need to take a look at what the variable is all about. A variable is basically a little container that is going to store information inside of the memory of the computer. You are able to use these to hold either one or more value of your choice, and you are able to assign this either at the beginning of your block of code or when the code is being executed.

Assigning a variable is going to be pretty easy to accomplish. You will just need to use the (=) in order to pick the value that you would like to use along with the variable. You are able to add more than one value to the same variable if you would like to store them together in the code, but for the most part, it is just going to be one variable that you are working with. You can add in many different variables inside of the code, but the operators that we are going to talk about in a minute help to make it easier to get this all done.

Before we get too far into making this kind of program, we are going to take some time to work with operators. While these are pretty simple, there are some times when they can seem confusing and will make you wonder what they mean. The trick with these is to not think of them as mathematical symbols. For example, when it comes to writing out a = 2, you should see this as the value of 2 is going to be stored inside the memory of your computer that is labeled as a. Here is another example that you can use:

a = 2

b = 3

c = a + b

In the statement that we did above, you will see that the value of 2 is going
to be stored as the memory location that is a and then you will see that the
value of 3 is stored in the memory location that is called be. And then when
you add the values of a and b together, you are going to store that result
under the memory location of c. Keep in mind with this one that you are
not able to write out this kind of equation as a + b = c because the compiler
is going to see this as an error. The one variable needs to be on the left-
hand side of your symbol and then you can have as many of the variables as
you would like on the right-hand side, but mixing these around are going to
cause an error message.

Arithmetic operators

Now that we have looked at some examples of operators, it is time to work
with some of the operators that you need. Not all of the math symbols that
you will need are going to show up on the keyboard, but the Fortran does
have some of its own symbols that you are able to use in order to represent
the different math operands that you are able to use. Some of the most
common arithmetic operators that you are able to use on your language
includes:

- (+): this is the one that you are going to use for addition
- (-): this is the one that you are going to use for subtraction in the
  code.
- (*): this is the one that you are going to use for multiplication
- (/): this is the one that you can use for division

One thing to note with these is that you can use more than one of the
symbols, whether you are using three addition signs or an addition and a
division symbol, inside the same part of code. You are able to use as many
of these as you want, but you need to use the order of operands to do it.
This means that you will need to do all of the multiplication, then the
division, addition, and subtraction, going from left to right to make sure
that the compiler is going to give you the right answer.

Other parts of your code

As a beginner, you will wonder what all the blanks, or the skip positions, are inside of the program. Some people choose to write out their programs without using these at all, but for the most part, the programmers like to include these inside of their code in order to make it easier to read. You are able to choose how you would like to use a skip position, but you should include at least a few to make sure that your code is easier to read through.

There are also some special characters that you are able to work with inside of your code. These are used in order to deliver the function that you want. These are going to seem pretty simple and plain but you need to be careful about how you use them. If you use them the wrong way or place two of them into the code right next to each other, you could end up with conditions that cancel each other. Some of the special characters that are found inside of Fortran and that you should watch out for include:

- (/): this one is going to specify another line
- (''): to output strings
- (:): this is going to terminate a list
- () this is going to categorize the descriptors.

Descriptors can be a tool that you are able to use and they are variables that are going to specify the amount of data that is required for a conversion. It is a good idea to keep track of the usage of these since the process may not end unless you add in the right descriptor is placed inside. Some of the descriptors that you can use include:

- A: repetition
- D: this one is for digits next to your decimal points.
- E: this is for an exponential number
- M: this is the minimum amount of digits.
- W: this is width in total characters.

You are going to be able to use all of these different parts to help you to get the code to work the way that you would like. You can mix and match a few of the parts to get the variable to be the right number, to store it in the right place inside the code and to do so much more. When you are able to add in the operators of the Fortran code, work with the blanks or the skip positions to make the code easier to use, and add in the special characters and the descriptors to the code, you are going to get a lot of power and options inside of the code.

Chapter 5: Working with Conditional Statements

At this point, we are going to take some time to look at the if statements. These are the most basic of the conditional statements and you will find that they are pretty straightforward. With this one, you will set the condition that needs to be met as well as the action that will show up at the same time with it. If the user puts in an input that matches, you will see that the program puts up the action that you choose. On the other hand, since this is a simple equation to work with, when the user puts in an input that is seen as false, the program is just going to end because you didn't set up an action.

So for this one, let's say that you just want people who are 18 to be able to get into the website. You would set up the if statement to accept any answer that is 18 and above. If the user places their age inside to be 20, the action (such a statement that you choose) will be executed by the compiler. But if the user puts in that their age is 16, then the program is going to see that this answer is false compared to the conditions that you set, and since you are using the if statement, nothing is going to happen.

Now there are some issues that can come up with this, but let's just focus on learning the syntax and getting this part down. Take a look at the syntax below for this:

```
if (x == 1) then

print *, 'turn left'

end if
```

The logical operator is the one that is used in this example along with the statement of if..then..end if. Note the expression that comes after the if statement. It is going to provide you with a test, something that is necessary when you are trying to imply a condition. In this case, we are going to assume that the "x" variable is an integer. One of the values that it can be is equal to 1. Interpreting this as a logical operation, the program is going to test to see if the value of the variable is 1. Then it will check if this is true or not. If your variable is 1, then the statements that come next will be executed which in this case would be the words "turn left". Then the end if is going to terminate the program that you are working on.

The if...else statements

As we mentioned in the last part, the if statement is going to be pretty basic
and there are some issues with it. Your user may very well be 16 years old
and it isn't a good idea to have the program just end if they put in this
answer. You most likely will want to have some message come up at least,
so that the user doesn't assume that something is wrong with the program.
For example, if they put that their age is over 18, you would want to set it
up to say something like "Welcome to the site!" and then have the next
action be that they can get in. But if they put in that they are 16 or
something else, you would rather have a message like "Only those over 18
are allowed in the game!" than having the program just end.

The if...else statement is able to help you to do that. You would set it up like
the first part that we had above, but then you would add the else that
catches anything that is considered false by the compiler based on the
conditions that you set. This allows you to have an answer, any answer,
come up regardless of what input the user is giving to you. This makes it
much more clean cut and easier to deal with and doesn't leave the user
wondering what is wrong with the user.

In addition, you are able to make it so that there are several options that
come up. Let's say that you would like to have someone pick out their
favorite color of either red, green, yellow, or blue. You would just need to
write out more of the else sections of this code would just keep going.
Another really useful thing for you to learn how to use inside of your
Fortran code is the conditional statement. These are really great because
they allow you to have some extra power and choices inside of the code.
These will allow you to put in the conditions that need to be met in order to
get different statements or actions to occur. They can be really simple, such
as the if statement, where you will only have an action happen when the
answer is inputted is true compared to your conditions, you can have it so
that a different action will happen based on if the answer is true or false
based on your condition, or you can give the user some choices.

You can decide what conditions need to be met before you allow the user to
put in their information. This allows the code to keep things simple and it
can look at your conditions before executing what you would like to have
happen. You can make these as complex or as simple as you would like, but
remember that you do need to base these on Boolean expressions. You

have to leave the answer as either true or false based on the conditions that
you set.

Don't worry if this sounds complicated right now. We are going to take
some time to look over the different conditional statements that you are
able to work with and help you to get the results that you want, no matter
what kind of conditional statement you are working with.

The if statements

down the line, taking a look through each condition and statement that you
put onto the screen. You can also add in a catch or break at the end so if the
user picks pink or another color that isn't listed there so they still get an
answer.

There are so many options that you are able to do with the if...else
statements and they can really open up a lot of what you are able to do
inside of your code. You can make them as simple or as complex as you
would like, adding in more sections or just having a true and false option.
Mess around with this a bit and see what you are able to come up with on
your if...else statements.

Conclusion

Working in a coding language can be difficult no matter who you are. Many beginners are worried that they are not going to be able to find the answers to getting started or that it is just going to be too hard for them to pick out how to work with this code. But when it comes to working in Fortran, you will find that writing out a code can be nice and simple and it won't take that long for you to learn it and start working on your own.

This guidebook is going to take some time to help you learn how to work with the Fortran code. We are going to start out with writing some of our own codes while learning about some of the basics that come with Fortran. We will then move on to working with strings and arrays, understanding how the loops work, and even working with conditional statements. These are actually really important parts of working with a coding language, but since Fortran is so simple to work with that you will be able to add them into a code in no time.

When you are ready to get started on writing some of your own codes and want to get into the world of coding, working with Fortran is one of the best options to help you to get this all done. It is an older language that is meant for beginners and you will be able to catch on to it in no time at all. Use this guidebook to learn what you need to know in order to get the Fortran language to work for you.

Book 2

Hacking

By: PG WIZARD BOOKS

Top Online Handbook in Exploitation of Computer Hacking, Security, and Penetration Testing!

Hacking: Top Online Handbook in Exploitation of Computer Hacking, Security, and Penetration Testing!

Table of Contents

Introduction

The world of hacking is an interesting world. Most of us only understand what is going on based on the movies that we watch or the news that we read about hackers stealing identities of those around them. These are parts of the whole hacking world, but there is so much more that comes with it. For example, some hackers are considered ethical hackers, which means that they are going to work to prevent others from getting onto their own systems, or the systems of others they are working for.

This guidebook is going to take some time to discuss the basics of the hacking world. We will start out with the difference between white hat hackers and black hat hackers and how each of them are going to work on the hacks that they are creating. We will then move on to working with how to map out your hack, especially if you want to check for vulnerabilities inside of your own system. And then the rest of the book will spend time looking at some of the common types of hacking that you can do including man in the middle hacks and even hacking passwords.

Even when it comes to hacking into a network that you are allowed to be on, it is important to learn how to do some basic hacks because you will be using the same methods that the black hat hackers are doing as well. This guidebook is going to help you to get started with doing some of the hacks that you need to ensure that you are getting the best results that you want.

Chapter 1: Some of the Basics of Computer Hacking

The process of hacking has gotten a bad name, mainly because of all the stories that have gone on in the media and in the movies about this topic. We may imagine someone who is just trying to get onto a system the are not allowed to be in or about someone who hacks into the government computers in order to get some important information and save the day. But there are many different facets that come up when we are talking about hacking and while some hackers are interested in stealing information and being places they aren't allowed to be, there are some who are more interested in learning hacking in order to protect their own computer systems and information.

There are two main types of computer hacking that you can come across. These include:

- Black hat hacking: this is the type that is found inside the movies. This is when someone tries to get onto a system that they don't belong, without the permission of the person who owns the system. Often this is done so that the hacker is able to get information they are not supposed to have, such as your personal information and credit card numbers.
- White hat hacking: this is the type of hacking that you may do when trying to keep your computer system and information safe from someone who may try to get the information and use it for their own reasons. Also, white hat hackers may also work with a big company, working on hacking on the system to see if it is vulnerable, in order to keep other people out of the system.

Both of these types of hackers are going to use the same methods to do the hacking, but the reasons behind the hacking are going to be completely different. It is important to note that black hat hacking is illegal and if you do this kind of hacking, it could end up with you going to jail and in a lot of trouble. But there is nothing wrong with hacking on to a system that you have permission to be on, such as your own personal computer, to help keep it safe or as part of your job.

Hacking: Top Online Handbook in Exploitation of Computer Hacking, Security, and Penetration Testing!

Penetration testing

Now that we have a little basics of the world of hacking, it is time to look more into the world of computer hacking. We will start this out with penetration testing. This is known as an authorized attempt in order to exploit a computer system in the hopes of learning the flaws that are inside of it so that you can work to make it more secure. When you are given the assignment to do a penetration test, or you decide to do it on your own system, you will be investigating the system in order to prove that there are vulnerabilities in the network.

After you are done with doing the penetration test, the mitigation measures will be made in order to address any of the issues that you found and fix the issues that you discovered during this test. It is basically a process of finding the threats that are present inside of the system and then come up with a good plan that is going to take care of the issues that show up during the test. Doing these on occasion to the system can ensure that you catch the vulnerabilities inside the system before someone else gets on and steals your information.

Penetration testing is also known as ethical hacking. There is a very thin line that is present between vulnerability assessment and penetration testing. These terms are often interchanged but they are not really the same thing. For example, the vulnerability assessment is going to be responsible for evaluations the system for any security issues that may be present already. But the penetration test is going to be the test that is used in order to exploit and also proves that these security issues exist. The test is going to allow the hacker to test out the system as an outside source so that they can see how the vulnerabilities are affecting things.

As a white hat hacker, you would want to go through the system and perform the same actions that a black hat hacker would do on the system in this kind of test. You would try to get onto the system to see how bad the vulnerabilities are and to determine what information others are able to see. While the black hat hacker would simply do this in the hopes of trying to get onto the system and exploit it for their own personal gains, you are going to find out where these things are and learn how to close them up. Even though both of you will use the same methods in order to get onto the system, you are going to have different reasons for getting onto the system.

A hacking lab

As a beginner to working on hacking, you may want to consider working in a hacking lab. This is a safe environment that you are able to work in with the attacks and the traffic to see how they respond to different things that you are working on, without them getting out of hand and heading to places they are not supposed to be. This is a good place for a beginner to get started with because it allows you to get some practice without ruining anything in the system or causing some issues. Once you get a little bit more of the practice into the thing, you will be able to move out of the hacking lab and have some fun with hacking, and do some of the tests, on a real network.

While there are some differences in the reason for hacking between a white hat and a black hat hacker, both of these groups are going to use the same kinds of skills and techniques in order to get the information that they want. The trick here is for the white hat hacker to know just as much, of not more, and to be faster at finding the vulnerabilities compared to the black hat hacker. This will help to keep the system protected and ensures that the other group isn't able to get information they are not supposed to have.

Chapter 2: Mapping Out the Hack Before Beginning

So before we get too far in this process, it is important to come up with the plan that you want to use. This is meant to give you a good idea of what you need to do and where you want to look for some of these vulnerabilities inside of your system. The strategies that you will use are important, but you really need to focus on having a good plan in place before you get too far in this process.

When you are trying to find some of the vulnerabilities that are needed, you don't need to waste your time checking all of the protocols for security at the same time. This can make it a bit confusing and sometimes it is going to make you deal with more problems than you want because too much information is coming towards you. This means that you should break your system up into parts and then test each of these parts so that the work is more manageable overall.

For the most part, it is a good idea to start out with the application or system that you are worried about the most, and then go down the list until you get to each of them. To help you to determine which of the systems you should work with first, consider these questions:

- If the system is attacked, which system or application is going to cause the most issues. Which one has the most information or would be the hardest to fix up if it were lost.
- If the system is attacked, which application is going to be the easiest for the hacker to get in to.
- Which sections of the system are you working on and are considered the least documented, which means that they are rarely checked. Do you notice some that you have never seen there before?

As you answer these questions, it is going to become easier to figure out which applications you should work on first and it is easier to go through the whole process and find the results that you want. There are many places that you are able to check out to make sure the tests are run the proper way including the routers and the switches, workstations and laptops, operating systems, databases and applications, firewalls, files, and emails servers and more. It is possible that you will need to run many tests to get all of these so take your time and try them out to see where the vulnerabilities may lie.

When should I do my hack?

Once you have a good list of the applications and devices that you want to check, the next question that you may have is when is a good time to hack. You will need to make sure that you complete the hacks during a time that is going to cause the least amount of disruption in the company or on your own personal computer. This means during the peak hours of the day, you should not be doing these hacks because they could potentially cause a lot of slow down and issues with the system and depending on the type of hack that you do, and if it goes well or not, it could even shut down the network when it is needed most. The best time to complete the tasks is when there is going to be minimal disruption, so coming in after hours is often best since few people will be on the system or the building could be closed and no one will even notice.

The time that works the best for these hacks will vary depending on the situation. For example, if you are doing one of these hacks on your own computer, the timing may not matter as much because you would just pick a time when you are free to do the hacks and call it good. On the other hand, if you are doing this as a job for your employer, you will need to abide by their busy times and pick one that is not going to interfere with the business, especially if the hack does cause some issues.

Will others see what I am doing?

When you are working on these hacks in order to find some of the vulnerabilities that are in the system, you need to think just like a criminal hacker would, since these are the type of people that would try to get onto the system. Sometimes being able to look at the system through fresh eyes can make all the difference. For example, when you are used to using this system, you are an insider and could have troubles seeing what is going on in the system, but it is important that you make sure that when you do the hacks, no one else is able to see what you are doing. The criminal hacker would be careful about who is able to notice their presence so you would want to be the same way.

Hacking: Top Online Handbook in Exploitation of Computer Hacking, Security, and Penetration Testing!

Now, it is your job to also check out what the hacker is able to see on your system. Hackers are always trying to find out as much information about the system as possible to make it easier to get onto it, and there are trails left all over the place for them to look at. As the ethical hacker of the system, it is your responsibility to find out what kind of information is out there for the other hackers to find and then learn how to diminish these trails to make your website and system harder to mess with. There are several different scanner types that you are able to use, such as a port scanner, so that you can see what information that is being shared, making it easier to catch some of these issues. Some of the other searches that you can do to protect your network includes doing a search online for the following information:

Any contact details. This is going to be information that can point back to the people connected with your business. Some options like USSearch and ChoicePoint are good ones to visit and see if your information is present there.

Look for any recent press releases that may talk about changes that have happened in the organization.

Look through any of the acquisitions and mergers of the company.

Always see if you can find any SEC documents about the company online.

Any patents or trademarks that are associated with this company.

Incorporation filings. These are also found through the SEC, but sometimes they are located elsewhere.

Be as thorough as possible about this point so that you have a good idea of what hackers are able to find out about your company or about your network. Often doing a keyword search is not going to bring up the results that you would like so you need to work with some advanced searches to find out all the information that you would like. At this point, you have a good idea of the different things that your computer or your network is sending out to other people and you can create the plan to get it all under control. Deleting information from online can help but running some port and network scans are great as well. Go through as many of these scans and tests as you can to help keep the computer network as safe as possible.

Chapter 3: Doing a Spoofing Attack

The first type of attack that we are going to explore is the spoofing attack. Whether you are working as a criminal hacker or as an ethical hacker, there are a lot of things that you can work with in order to get into a system that you shouldn't be on. As a hacker, you are responsible for researching and having some patience to wait in order to find the vulnerability that is on the system or network before taking the next move. But with the right kind of work, it is easier to get on the network and often a few different options are going to show up for you. One method that you can use is the spoofing technique that allows you to convince the computer system that you should be there so that you can get all the information that you want. Let's take a look at how this works and how you can make it happen with your hacking.

Spoofing

One of the first techniques that we are going to explore in this guidebook is spoofing. This is basically going to be a technique where the hacker is able to pretend that they are another person, software, website, or organization in order to convince the network that they are supposed to be here. The hacker is meant to look like this other person so that the network will allow them through the security protocols and then the hacker can get through where they want, get the information that is needed, and even leave the system before anyone else is able to see them. There are a few options that you are able to pick from when it comes to the spoofing technique including:

IP spoofing

With the technique of IP spoofing, the hacker is going to mask up their IP address or make changes to it so that the network things that the hacker belongs to the network. The hacker is able to make these changes so that the IP address either matches up with what is allowed on the network or it is one that the network is going to be familiar with. With this method, the hacker is able to be in any part of the world that they want, but the network is still going to allow them to get on because the IP address matches up in some manner. Once the hacker is able to get on to the system, they have the ability to take over this network, change files, delete things, and do some other tasks without ever being detected.

If the hacker is able to pull off this technique, it is very successful because it has convinced the network that the hacker is supposed to be there. The trusted IP address is found by the hacker and then it is used to get onto the network and make the changes that are needed. The hacker will be able to use this in order to gain full access to the whole system, whether they choose to sit around and wait for a good opportunity or they choose to do an attack and get the information they want right away.

DNS spoofing

Another spoofing technique is known as DNS spoofing. This method is going to trick a user who is trying to get onto a legitimate site. The hacker will take the IP address and then when a user clicks on it, they will be sent to a malicious website where the hacker has complete control. Sometimes the hacker will take over a legitimate website and turn it to their use, but often they will change around a letter or two to trick people. Users who aren't paying attention or who type in the address wrong will be sent to a bad website and the hacker can take credentials and private information from the user.

Often the user will not realize that they are being tricked. They will get onto the website and figure that it is just where they want to be. They can put in private information, send payment, and more while the hacker is collecting it all privately.

For the hacker to get this to work, they need to have the same LAN as their target. This requires the hacker to search for a weak password on one of the machines that is on the network, something that is possibly even from a different location. Once the hacker accomplishes this, they will be able to redirect all users to their website and easily monitor the activities that are done there.

Email spoofing

Email spoofing is one of the most common types of spoofing, which is one of the reasons that people should be very careful about the emails that they are receiving, sending, and clicking on. This can be a useful technique when the hacker wants to try and get past some of the security that is placed on email accounts. Most email servers are going to be good at recognizing if someone looks like they are legitimate and when something is spam, but there are also times when the hacker will be able to get past this and can send malicious attachments.

The most common form of this is when the hacker is able to pretend to be someone else inside the system so that they can intercept the emails from both parties, either read them or make changes, and then send the emails on without either of the two parties knowing. This can be really useful to the hacker because they can really get stuff done, and get ahold of private information that might be hidden elsewhere.

Phone number spoofing

When it comes to using phone number spoofing, the hacker is going to get ahold of some false numbers, or even area codes, so that they can mask their location. This is the best way for the hacker to be able to get into some of the voicemail messages that you have, and even to send out some text messages using this number. The target is often misled about where the hacker is from. Often this one is used when the hacker wants to pretend that they belong to a government office to trick the target.

The spoofing attacks can be difficult because often the network administrator is not even able to find out these attacks. The hacker will be able to stay on the network and cause almost as much damage as they want to these systems, without ever being found. It is often only after the hacker causes a big mess or when important information is leaked out that the hacker is finally caught and taken off the system. The hacker will be able to use just these kinds of hacks or some of the others in order to get the results they want and often they will be undetected by others on the same network.

Chapter 4: Man in the Middle Attacks

In addition to being able to do the spoofing attacks that we talked about in the previous chapter, it is also possible for a hacker to do a man in the middle attack. Sometimes the hacker will do this as a passive attack in order to just get on the system and see what information they are able to get, and other times they will use an active attack to get information, slow down the system, or cause some other form of problems.

When it comes to the man in the middle attacks, the hacker is able to do this with a form of spoofing that is called Address Resolution Protocol, or ARP. With this, the hacker is able to send messages that are false, but which are going to look normal, all over the network that they are working on. When it is pulled off, these fake messages allow the hacker to link up with another IP address of one of the users on the network. Once the hacker is done with this part, they can receive any of the data that all of the users are sending with this IP address and use it in the way that they would like.

So basically with this, the hacker is taking over an IP address and making it their own. They will receive all files, communication, and other information that is meant to go to the original user and they can use it however they would like. The hacker has the ability to get onto the network while receiving all traffic that goes on the network as well.

1. Session hijacking—this is when the hacker will use their false ARP to still the user's ID for the session. The hacker will be able to hold on to the information about the traffic and use it at a later date to get access to the account.

2. Denial of service attack—this is an attack done when the ARP spoof links several IP addresses to the target. During this attack, the data that should be sent to the other IP addresses are sent to one device. This is going to result in an overload of data.

3. Man in the middle attack—with this attack, the hacker is going to pretend that they are non-existent inside the network. Since they are hidden, they are able to modify and intercept messages that are sent between two or more users on the network. The one network may send a legitimate email, but the hacker will take it and change the information to be more

malicious before sending it on. The second user will open the malicious information, believing it to be safe.

Now that we know a bit more about a man in the middle attack, you are probably interested in learning some of the steps that are needed in order to complete the man in the middle attack. Here are some of the options that you can use and we are going to bring in the tool called Backtrack in order to get this done:

Do the research

The first step that you will need to do is find out the data that is needed to begin. The tool Wireshark is a good one to work with because it will help you to get all of this information to get on to the system. Firing up this tool on the network is going to allow the hacker to see what traffic is able to get onto the network through either the wireless or wired networks and is a really good place to get started for an access point.

Use your wireless adapter in monitor mode

Now that we have done some research, it is time to work with the wireless adapter and change it over to what is known as the monitor mode. This mode is going to make it easier for you to see the traffic that goes into your connection, even the traffic that isn't allowed to be there. This method is the one that you will work when using hubbed networks because you will find that the hubbed ones won't have as much security as you will find with the switched networks.

If you are able to see what information is going between the users that are on the switch, or you would like to make a bypass over this completely, you are able to work on making changes to the entries that are inside of your CAM table that is responsible for mapping out the IP and MAC addresses that are sending information to each other. When you are able to make changes to these entries, it is easier to get ahold of this traffic, make changes or at least read through it, and then send it back on without others knowing. The ARP spoofing attack is going to make this easier to accomplish.

Turning on backtrack

Now that you have changed the adapter and gotten it set up the way that you would like, it is time to fire up the Backtrack that you would like to use. You will need to pull up the Backtrack and then pull up all three terminals. Next, you will replace the MAC address from the target client with your personal MAC address. The code for doing this is: arpspoof [client IP] [server IP].

Once you do that, you will need to reverse the order of the IP addresses in the string that you just used. This is going to tell the server that your computer is the authorized one so that you are allowed to get onto the system and perform other tasks. You are basically going to become the server and the client so you can receive packets of information and change them how you wish. It also goes the other way around.

For those who are using Linux, you can use the built in feature known as ip_forward, which will make it easier to forward the packets you are receiving. Once you turn this feature on, you will be able to go back into Backtrack and forward these packets with the commandecho 1 >/proc/sys/net/ipv4/ip_forward.

This command is going to make it easier to be right between the client and the server. You will get all the information that goes between these two and as the hacker, you can use the information as you wish. You could look at the system, take personal information, or change anything you want about information that is shared.

Check out your traffic

At this point, you should be able to get access to all of the information that the users are all sending through the network. You will get to be right in the front row of this action and you can either watch the information that is being sent or grab ahold of some of it and make changes before sending it all back through the system again. You can use your BackTrack tool in order to sniff out the traffic and get a nice clear picture of the system. You need to take some time to activate this feature in order to make it work, but it can make things easier to work with.

Get your data as well as the credentials

Now you will just need to wait around and see when the client is logging into the server. Once the client logs on, you will be able to see their username and password coming up right in front of you. This means that the information is going to be right in front of you, making it easier to record and use it whenever you would like. Since the users and the administrators are all going to use these same credentials on all of the systems on the computer, you can keep using these credentials in order to get anywhere that you would like. You are now right in the middle of all the information on the system and you can use it in any manner that you would like, without other users on the system having any idea.

And now you are done creating your very first man in the middle attack. This is a great way for you to get in the middle of the all the action on a system, and the other users will have no idea that you are there. There are many things that you are able to do from here, such as intercepting information, changing the messages that are sent, slowing down the system, and even getting ahold of some classified information. this can really put the hacker right in the middle of the action so it is a great way for you to get started.

Hacking: Top Online Handbook in Exploitation of Computer Hacking, Security, and Penetration Testing!

Chapter 5: How to Use Hacking to Get Passwords

The biggest target of hackers is to get passwords, mainly because they are really easy to get. Most people think that they just need to come up with a longer password in order to protect themselves, but there is more to it than that. If the hacker is able to use some of the tricks we stated earlier in this chapter, it does not matter how long your username and password is, they will still have it sent directly to them.

Confidential log in information, including passwords, are considered the weakest links in security because the only thing it relies on is secrecy. Once the secret is out, the security is pretty much gone. This is why it is such a big deal when a big company is hacked and all the username and passwords are leaked. The hacker is now able to get onto the system and use your information however they wish. Sometimes, the user themselves will inadvertently give out their own password for hackers to use.

So how do you hack a password? There are several ways that the hacker can do this including a physical attack, social engineering, and inference. There are also a few different tools that are used to crack passwords including:

1. Cain and Abel—this one is good to help with Windows RDP passwords, Cisco IOS hashes and more.

2. Elmcomsoft Distributed Password Recovery—this one is able to get PGP and Microsoft Office passwords and has been used in order to crack distributed passwords as well as recover up to 10,000 networked computers.

3. Elmcomsoft System Recovery—this has the ability to set administrative credentials, rest expirations on passwords, and reset passwords on Windows computers.

4. Ophcrack—this will use rainbow tables to crack passwords for Windows.

5. Pandora—this can be a good one to use to crack Novell Netware accounts either online or offline.

Some of these tools do have a shortfall because they will require the hacker to have physical access to the system they are hacking. But once the hacker has access to the system that you are protecting, they will be able to dig into all of your encrypted and password protected files with just a few tools.

Hacking: Top Online Handbook in Exploitation of Computer Hacking, Security, and Penetration Testing!

Often, the hacker is not going to have access to your computer to do a password hack and they will rely on some other tools. Some examples of other methods used to hack a password include:

1. Dictionary attacks—these are attacks that will make use of dictionary words against the password database. This makes it easier to figure out if there is a weak password in the system.

2. Brute force attacks—these are capable of cracking all types of passwords because they are going to use all combinations of numbers, special characters, and letters until the device is cracked. The biggest flaw with this technique is that it can take a ton of time to uncover the password.

3. Rainbow attacks—these are good for cracking any hashed passwords. The tool is really fast compared to others, but it is not able to uncover passwords that are more than 14 characters.

4. Keystroke logging—this is one of the best techniques for cracking a password because it is asking the targeted computer to basically send over the information. The hacker is able to place a recording device on the targeted system to take in all the keystrokes done on the computer. The information is then sent over using programs such as KeyGhost.

5. Searching for weak storages—there are a lot of applications in computers that will store the passwords locally, making them vulnerable to a hacker. When you have physical access to the computer, it is easy to find the passwords through text searches and sometimes they are even stored on the application.

6. Grab the passwords remotely—often it is not possible to physically access a system, it is still possible to get the passwords from a remote location. You will need to do a spoofing attack first, exploit the SAM file and have the information sent to you.

Once the hacker has access to these passwords, it is easier for them to get the information that they want. They can use the passwords to get onto the network, to get to emails, find out financial accounts, and so much more. You must remember that passwords are a huge vulnerability in your system and to figure out more secure ways to protect your system.

Chapter 6: Getting Through Internet Connections for the Hack

If you would like to work on hacking online, you will need to learn how to get through the internet connection, as well as the security features, that are found online. Here we are going to talk about how to hack through a WEP connection as well as how to perform an evil twin hack so that you can check to see if your system is susceptible to this kind of attack or not:

How to hack a WEP connections

While there are a few different types of internet connections that you can work with in order to hack, this is one of the easiest to go through. If this is the one that your system is working with, you will definitely need to run through a few tests to see if you have been hacked or if you can make it more secure. Some of the things that you will need to check and hack through a WEP connection includes:

1. To get started, load up the BackTrack and the aircrack-ng. you can fire up BackTrack and then make sure that it is plugged into the wireless adapter to see if it is running. You can type in lwconfi in order to see if this is working. The program is then going to tell you which of the adapter it can recognize and if this is working properly, it is going to see yours.

2. Then take the wireless adapter and set it so it is at promiscuous mode. This will allow you to see what other connections are available and you can type in "airmon-ng start wlano" in order to do this. You can then change the name of your interface to have it read momo. You now have the adapter inside of monitor mode and you can type in "airodump-ng mono" to see which access points are available and what is attached to them.

3. Start capturing your access point. You will need to pick which connection you want to get on and then capture it. You can do this by using the command

    a. Airodump-ng –bssid [BSSID of target] -c [channel number] -w WEPcrack momo.

    b. Once you enter this command, the BackTrack is going to start capturing packets fro the access point on the right channel. This will send the hacker all the packets that it needs in order to decode any passkeys that are present so they can get onto the wireless. However, it is important to realize that getting these packets will often take some time. If you need to get the packets quickly, it may be time to add in an ARP traffic.

4. Inject the ARP traffic—for anyone who doesn't want to wait around for the packets from WEPkey capture, doing an ARP packet and having it replay can help you get the packets that you need to crack the WEPkey. Since you already have the MAC and BSSID address from the target thanks to doing step 3, you will be able to use them to enter the following command:

   a. Aireplay-ng -3 -b [BSSID] – [MAC address] mono

   b. This will allow you to capture the ARPs through the access point of the target. You must keep going in order to capture the IVs that will come in as well.

5. Crack the WEPkey. Once you have the necessary amount of IVs in your WEPcrack file, it is time to run your aircrack-ng. Put in the command:

   a. Aircrack-ng [name of file]

   b. The aircrack-ng will enter the passkey in a hexadecimal format. You will just need to apply this key into your remote access point and then you are on the program. You can use it for free internet, to take over a computer on the system, and much more.

The Evil Twin Hack

The evil twin hack is an access point that will act like the access point that a user connects to, but it is manipulative. The target will just see their regular access point and think it is safe to get on, but this manipulative access point is used by a hacker to send the target to the hackers' premade access point, where the hacker can then start a dangerous man in the middle attack.

As a beginner hacker, you may need some practice doing the evil twin attack. Some basic steps to try out include:

1. Turn on BackTrack and start the program airmon-ng. Check to see if your wireless card is running properly by entering bt>iwconfig.

2. Once you have the wireless card, it is time to put it into monitor mode. You will be able to do this by entering the command bt >airmon-ng start wlan0.

3. Now you need to fire up the airdump-ng. you will start capturing the wireless traffic that your wireless card is able to detect. To do this, enter

the command bt >airodump-ng mono. After this step, you will have the ability to see all access points that are in range and can pick out the one that belongs to your target.

4. You will need to wait for when the target connects. Once the target gets onto the access point, you can copy the BSSID and the MAC address that you want to hack into.

5. Now the hacker will need to create an access point that has the same credentials.

   a. First, pull up a new terminal and type in bt > airbase-ng -a [BSSID] –essid ["SSID of target] -c [channel number] mono

   b. This is going to create the access point that you want. It will look the same as the original access point so the target will click on it, but it puts the hacker right in the middle as the one in control.

6. De-authenticate the target—for the target to get onto your new access point, you will need to get them off the one they are connected to. Since many wireless connections will go with 802.11, everyone who is connected to the access point will be de-authenticated when you do this. When the target tries to get back on to the internet, they will connect automatically to the one with the strongest signal, which in this case will be your manipulated access point.

   a. To get the target off their access point, make sure to do the following command: bt > aireplay-ng –deauth 0 -a [BSSID of target]

7. Turn the signal of the evil twin up. The trick on this one is to get the fake access point to have a strong signal. It needs to be at least as strong, but preferably stronger, than the original point of access. This can be tricky because you are likely further away than the original access point.

   a. Iwconfig wlano txpower 27 will help you to turn up the signal on your access point.

   b. This can add 500 milliwatts to your power. If you are too far away though, this may not be enough. You either need to be closer to the target or consider a newer wireless card that is able to go up to 2000 milliwatts.

8. Put the evil twin to good use—once you have established the evil twin and you know that the target and the network are all connected to it, it is time to take the steps needed in order to detect all the activities going on in the system. It often depends on what you want to do with the system for where you will go from here.

a. There are a lot of options of what to do at this point. Hackers who have gone and created an evil twin are interested in more than just free wireless so they will often do man in the middle attacks, intercept traffic, add in new traffic, or steal information from the system, often without the target realizing.

Conclusion

Working in the world of hacking can be really interesting. There are a lot of people who are interested in knowing how to protect their own systems from a hacker getting on and finding out information that they shouldn't, but most of us assume that going through the process of hacking is going to be too difficult to get started. But with the help of this guidebook, we are going to be able to learn some of the basics of working in hacking and how to protect your own network easily.

Inside this guidebook, we spent some time talking about the different ways that you are able to work with hacking. We started with some of the basics of hacking, such as the differences between white hat hackers and the black hat hackers and discussed how they often use some of the same methods to get things done. In addition, we talked about working on mapping your attack so that you have a plan and how to work with spoofing, man in the middle attacks, password hacks, and even how to hack through different connections online. All of these can come together to help you understand how to do a good hack and keep things safe from a hacker.

It is important that you learn how to keep your information safe from others who will try to get on your network and steal it. This guidebook is going to teach you some more about hacking and how you can use it for your needs and to keep your computer system safe.

Book 3

Android Crash Course

By: PG WIZARD BOOKS

Step by Step Guide To Mastering Android Programming!

Android Crash Course: Step by Step Guide To Mastering Android Programming!

Table Of Contents

Introduction

Working with the Android operating system can be a great experience. Unlike some of the other coding languages and operating systems out there, Android is the language that you will work with for mobile devices rather than for your computer. With that being said, you are still able to work on the computer, using an emulator, so that you can check out if the app that you create is going to work properly or not.

If you are interested in creating some of your own apps with the help of the Android operating system, this is the guidebook that is going to help you to get it done. It is a simple program to learn how to use, and this guidebook is going to make it easier than ever to get started. We will talk about some of the basics of working with the Android operating system as well as how it is all set up for you to use. Once that is done, we are going to learn how to download the Android operating system, set up the emulator, write your first code, and even make some changes to it later on. There is so much that you are able to do with the help of this operating system and we are going to take a look at some of the best parts of it with this guidebook.

When you are ready to learn a new coding language for your mobile devices, and you want to be able to create some of your own applications, make sure to check out this guidebook for the basics on how to get started from doing updates, to installing the software and even creating some of your first programs.

Chapter 1: An Overview of Android

If you are someone who likes to work in programming and even on smartphones, then the Android operating system is a great option for you to use. Android is an operating system that is based off Linux, which makes it really easy for you to use. The user interface is considered as direct manipulation based and it is one that will be used and designed to work with tablets and smartphones that are touchscreens as well as cars, televisions, and wristwatches that are compatible with this technology. With the operating system, you are able to make use of the touch inputs which will be able to correspond with actions that are done in the real world, such as pinching, swiping, and tapping.

With all of the things that Android is able to work with, you are going to find many different projects that you are able to create. Android is a really low-cost operating system that is ready made and can be customized to the needs that you have. And since it is able to be used with other high-tech devices, it has become really popular with a wide range of technology companies. Add in that this is an open source operating system (which means that programmers are able to use it and make changes as they see fit), it is easy to use on your own projects, and you can even find a large community of developers who can help you out.

There are many features that you are going to find with the Android system. You will be able to use it with other languages to work on your device, it has the power that you need to compete with the Apple operating system and Windows 8.1 it is able to store all the information that you need, works with your Wi-Fi, and even has an interface that is intuitive for the user. These are some of the features that you can enjoy while using the Android operating system and with the new innovations that are always coming out thanks to this code being open sourced, you are sure to find other benefits that will help you to get your projects done.

Android is one of the best-operating systems out there for devices like tablets, televisions, and mobile phones. There are billions of these devices hooked up to the Android system, and it has quickly become one of the largest mobile platform bases with a huge growth potential in the future. In fact, according to the Google Corporation, it is believed that more than a million new devices are activated with Android each day.

Android Crash Course: Step by Step Guide To Mastering Android Programming!

The interface

By default, the user interface in Android is going to be base don the touch inputs of the user with options like pinching, swiping, and tapping on the objects, or the keyboard on the screen of the device. So basically this is an operating system that is designed to respond to the input of the user right away, and it includes a smooth touch interface to make things easier. You will also find that this operating system is going to put to use the vibration feature of the device, so the user is able to get some haptic feedback.

The internal hardware that comes with this operating system, such as accelerometers, gyroscopes, and proximity sensors are used by the applications, and you can use it for adjusting the orientation of the screen, using remote controls, and even change up the home screen for the different pages that you use. Basically, this is a very intuitive interface that the user is going to love because it responds to their touches and it has so many different options that they are able to use.

Managing the memory

For the most part, the devices that run on Android are going to use battery. So if you want to make sure that the battery life is going to last longer, you will want to have a RAM that will consume less power because they will not get a continuous source of power like some of your desktop devices. Whenever the app is minimized, or it isn't in use, it is going to be placed inside the memory automatically. Yes, these applications are going to be open still, but this method is going to help to prevent it from consuming all the resources of the system; they will simply wait in the background until you decide to call them back up.

This is great for the Android device because you will be able to call it back up as needed, but it helps to save the limited RAM that you have. The RAM is limited because you want to make sure that it doesn't waste out all the battery power that you have this device. Luckily, this system is going to be good at managing some of your applications. If it notices that your memory is running low, it is simply going to terminate the processes that aren't being used, closing up the oldest applications first to save room.

Security and privacy

Many people are worried about getting on a new operating system is whether it is going to keep your privacy safe and if it is secure enough to work on the apps with. There are many operating systems that promise to be amazing when it comes to your security and privacy, but some of them may fall short at some times and won't provide the benefits that you are looking for. But when it comes to the Android operating system, you are going to get all the benefits of a lot of security and privacy, simply by the way that the system is set up to deal with the work that you are doing and since you get to determine how all the apps interact on the computer and get to give each of them permission before they get any information, you know that your privacy is always going to be safe.

The applications that you use in Android are going to run inside the sandbox, which is basically an area of your system that is isolated and will not have access to the other resources unless you give permission for this when you install the application. Before you install a new application, you will also need to give permission in order to get it on the system. This is going to take a bit more time through the installation process, but it helps to prevent bugs in the applications, limits documentation, and helps to keep your information secure and private no matter what.

Works with different languages

One of the nice things about working with the Android operating system is that it is able to work with many other coding languages. Almost all of the major coding languages are supported on these devices, and the list is currently at over 100 languages. This makes it easy for the Android device to adapt to what you want to use. It also supports Java so that if you want to create something to work online, the Java language is going to be easy to use.

These are just some of the things that you are going to fall in love with when you get started on the Android platform. It is great to work with mobile devices, no matter what kind you have, it has a lot of speed and stability so that you know that your coding will work out well, and you can develop many different kinds of applications, in many different coding languages if you want, without too much hassle.

The benefits of working with the Android operating system

Android Crash Course: Step by Step Guide To Mastering Android
Programming!

When it comes to working with an operating system that works out well with your mobile devices, none of them are going to be as great as the Android operating system. There are other options, but the Android operating system is going to work on billions of devices all over the world. Some of the benefits that you will be able to enjoy with this operating system include:

- Easy to use: working with the Android operating system can be really easy. You are going to learn how to create some of your own apps in no time, and then you can bring out your own creativity to work with Android or to create the apps that you dream about.
- Works well with mobile devices: the whole idea of using the Android operating system is so that you are able to use it to create apps that are good for your mobile devices. This can include things like televisions, tablets, and smartphones. You can use the emulator that is available for your computer, or your own device, in order to create an app and then have a chance to try it out to see if it works.
- Works with the Java language: you will need to know how to work with the Java language if you want to work on an Android app. This is a basic website and online building language that is easy to use, but it is important that you learn how to use this ahead of time.
- Allows you to create and sell your own apps: one of the reasons that a lot of people will choose to go with the Android operating system is because they have some ideas for apps that they want to use and hope to sell. There are millions of people who use the Android operating system on their devices, and they are always looking for new apps and games to work with. Some people choose to sell the apps for free, and others will make money off of the added space they sell or the cost of the app. This is a great way to make some extra money if you like to work with apps.
- The user interface is easy to work with: this user interface is meant to be really interactive. In fact, it is going to work mainly by the user working with their hands and fingers rather than relying on buttons and clicks like the other operating systems that you may be used to. This can make it easier for you to learn how to make apps that the customer will love because they can work on it in real time without all the extras going on around it causing it to be slower.
- A big community to ask questions with: the Android system has a big community of people you are able to meet with, ask questions of, and so much more when you need help. Android has been around for a long time,

and it has a lot of devices that will use this system to get things done. This
makes it easier for you to use the operating system and to get it to work the
way that you would like.

There are many options that you can choose when it comes to making a mobile
operating system work for your app. Some people will use the Windows system
and other times you will want to go with the Apple iOS. But none have the wide
range and all the flexibility that you need from the Android operating system, and
this is why so many people choose to go with it. With billions of devices that use
this operating system and a million more being added each day, it is no wonder
that people love being able to use and learn how to use Android.

Chapter 2: The Architecture of the Android Operating System

Before we get too far into developing our programs with the Android operating system, it is important to know some of the architecture that comes with this program and where things will work together. The framework of the application is easier to understand if we know how things are going to be arranged and will work inside of the operating systems. Since this is an operating system that is based on Linux, you will see that the two are very similar if you have worked with Linux in the past. For those who have never worked on Linux at all, you will notice that the layout of the language is pretty simple to use and you will catch on pretty quickly. Let's take a look at the architecture of this operating system.

Basic applications

The first applications that you are going to see are the basic ones. These are some of the options like the application to make calls, for your music player and camera and more. They don't have to come from Google, and sometimes Google isn't going to provide them at all, but you will be able to use the Google play store in order to develop these kinds of applications and make it so that they are available for everyone to use. You can also develop the apps with Java and then install them into the device that will integrate with the Android operating system.

Application framework

This is the part of the system that is going to be used for developing the applications. This framework is available with many different interfaces, and the developers will pick out which interface they want to use based on the standards that are important to them. By using these frameworks, you are going to save a lot of time and effort because it is not necessary to code out all of the tasks. There are also some different entities that come with the framework, and the options available are going to change based on the framework that you want to use.

Android Crash Course: Step by Step Guide To Mastering Android
Programming!

Activity manager

When you are using the activity manager, you are using the part of the program that is responsible for managing the different activities that control the app life cycle. It is going to have many different states, and the activity manager will be able to handle all of these. The applications are going to consist of many different types of activities, and each of these activities is going to have its own life cycle. Whenever you launch up a new application, one main activity is going to be started. You will be able to pull up a window when needed in order to see every activity inside an app.

Resource managers

If you have some applications that are going to require some kind of external resources, such as an external string, these are going to be managed with the help of your resource manager. These parts are going to be able to allocate the resources in the way that is standard for your device and will make sure that everything works together well.

Libraries

There are several libraries that you are able to us in Android in order to make sure that you are using the right codes, to save time, and to make your work more powerful. All of the native libraries for Android are going to be found inside of this layer, but all of them are going to be written using either the C++ or the C language. The capabilities that are found inside these libraries are going to be similar to what you find in the application layer on the top of the Linux kernel. Some of the things that you are going to find inside of these libraries on Android will include:

- Surface manager: this is the compositing window in manager and display.
- System C libraries: these are the basic libraries of C that are going to be targeted for the ARM or embedded devices.
- A media framework: this could include options for playback, recording, video, audio, and more.

- OpenGL ES libraries: this is the one that is needed for the graphics on the device.
- SQLite: this is a database engine. This one, in particular, is a smaller version that works better on Android without using up as much memory space.

All of these are going to come together in order to help you to find out the codes that you would like to use inside your program. You can use these as a simple way to get started on the app that you would like to use or as some suggestions as to what you would need to do next. You can always add in some of the other parts that you would like if the code really needs it, but this is one of the best places to start as a beginner in order to get your basics down and to start writing some of your own code.

Android Runtime

You will find that the Dalvik Virtual Machine is the part that is in charge of the runtime for all Android devices. This is a virtual machine that is going to be used for your embedded devices as well as an interpreter for bytecode. They are going to have lower memories and can be a bit slower than you are used to since they run on batteries. You will find that the Java libraries are also going to be on these devices which means that you will be able to use them.

Kernel

When it comes to using the Android operating system, you will be using the Linux Kernel 2.6. This is going to include all the electronic equipment that you need, and many of the processes are going to be similar to what you will find with the Linux operating system to make things easier. Between the software and hardware of Android, you are going to see that the kernel will behave similar to the abstraction layer in the hardware and will include essential parts like the keypad, camera, and display. The kernel is also going to be in charge of handling things like the networking and device drivers.

Keep in mind that working with the Linux system means that everything is going to be in the form of a kernel. This helps to add in some security to the system and makes the whole program easier to use. If you have ever worked with the Linux system, you are used to how easy the Linux operating system is to do a lot of different tasks, and this is going to translate over to the work that you are doing over on the Android operating system as well.

Now that you know a bit more about the different parts that come with the Android operating system and how it does work quite well with the Linux system, it is time to move on to downloading this software properly and working on a few of your very first projects to make things easier.

Chapter 3: Working on Your First Project

Now that we have taken the time to learn more about the Android system, it is
time to work on our first project. This one is going to be pretty simple to learn,
but will help you to get a feel for how all of this works for some of the other topics
we will bring up later on. But the first step that we need to take when getting
started is to install the Android Studio.

To start with this, we need to see if the Java Development Kit, or the JDK, is
installed on your computer or not. Some computers come with this already in
place so that can save you time. For a PC, you need to click on Start, Run, type in
the word "cmd" and then press enter to see if it is there. If you are on a Mac
computer, you will use the Spotlight to search for the Terminal and then choose
the top result. If this is on the computer, use the prompt "java-version." If a
command is not found, you will need to visit the Oracle website and download
the JDK on your computer.

Once this is done, it is time to go online and download the right version of the
Android Studio for your computer. When this has had time to download the right
way on the computer, you can click on Next to move on to the following screen.
At this location, you will need to pick the setup that you want to use (standard is
usually the best one) before clicking on Next and accepting the license
agreements. At this point, the Android Studio is going to finish up the download,
and you are ready.

For each version of Android that you are using, you will find that it contains a
version of SDK for you to work with. The setup wizard is going to help you to get
the updated versions of this. It is important to have the SDK because it helps you
to set up the Android Virtual Device, the part that allows you to test your new
apps on it and you can give it the right customizations for your own personal
configuration.

So go back to the Welcome Screen of the Android Studio and click Configure. You
should see a new menu that offers you a lot of options, and you will want to pick
the one that says SDK Manager. A new window should appear when you click on
this, and a series of folders, checkboxes, and statuses are going to show up. If you
just downloaded the Android Studio, you should have the latest version of SDK

Android Crash Course: Step by Step Guide To Mastering Android Programming!

Tools as well as some of the other tools to make the program work. If you see that an update is still available for this, the box will be ticked, and you can choose whether or not you want to take this.

Once you have had time to get the latest version of the SDK Manager on your computer (taking the time to update it if you need), it is time to create one of your first programs inside of the Android operating system.

Creating the OMG Android

Now it is time to start working on your very first project, and we are going to start out pretty simple, using the Hello, World! Kind of idea that the other coding languages go with. The idea behind this one is to give you some options and familiarity with using Android so that you can do some of the bigger projects later on.

The nice thing that you will notice about the Android Studio is that it comes with a nice tool that will give you the steps that you need to get this project started. You will just need to get on the Welcome Screen, click that you want to start a New Android Studio Project, and then the screen for project creation will show up. You are allowed to place an application name, and we are going to call this one OMG Android. For the company domain just put in your name. You may notice that the Package Name is going to change at this time to make a reverse domain name based on what you call the application and your company. This is going to be like a unique identifier so that the app is easily found among all the others.

Set the project location to the hard drive location that you would like before clicking on Next. On this screen, you are going to tell the system which devices and operating systems you would like to make the app work with. You probably don't want to make an app that will work with each Android device, but you can narrow this down to just smartphones or just tablets if you would like. For this one, to keep things easier, we are going to target the Android phone (you should see that this is the default option selected along with the Minimum SDK).

You can then click on Next to get to the following screen to choose what activity will happen for the app. A good way to think about this is as a window inside the

Android Crash Course: Step by Step Guide To Mastering Android Programming!

app that will be able to show what content will be interactive with the user. You can use this activity as a popup or as the while window. Inside of this template, the activities are going to range from being blank with an Action Bar all the way to one that has an embedded Map View. But for this project, we are going to keep things simple and work with Blank Activity before clicking Next.

At this point, you are almost to the coding. We are going to go through and use the default options with this and then click on the Finish button. There will be a few minutes for the Studio to go through and finish off the project and sometimes you will notice that it is going through all the different steps and putting out information about what it is doing. The nice thing is that with this IDE, a lot of work is going to be done for you.

After a few minutes, the Studio is going to finish building up this project. This project so far is going to be empty since we didn't put in any code to it, but it will contain all the information that is needed to be launched on one of the Android devices. At this point, you should see that there are three windows that are open on the Android Studio. On the left is going to be the project folder, the middle will have a preview of what this looks like on the Nexus 5, and then the last window is going to show the layout of the project.

Right now the project is pretty empty and will not show much up on the screen, but you will be able to make changes to that later on and add in some words as well as some other really cool things. But for now, you have created a good program so let's take that a step further in the next chapter and not only add in some of the words or phrases that you need to work with inside this operating system, but also learn how to make the app run with your emulator or with the Android   device.

66

Chapter 4: Running the App

So in the last chapter, we spent some time making a pretty basic app. We learned how to get it all setup and that the Android Studio is really great at setting the defaults that you want to use and which will ensure that you have it named the right way and ready to go. But so far the app doesn't have any words in it for others to see or any other actions, and it isn't running in a way that the other Android apps will be able to use. This chapter is going to take some time to add in these two options so that you can make your app start to work.

Running the app on an Emulator

So with the example that we did in the previous chapter, we took the time to create our first app, but now we need to figure out how to run that. If you already own an Android device, you are able to use this to run and test out the app, but if you don't have a device, you can choose to work with an emulator. The Android Studio is going to include the abilities that you need to set up a software-based device right on your computer. This basically means that you can run apps, debut the app, and look through a website on your computer, but it will work as if you were on the Android app. You will be able to set up as many emulators on your computer, and you can mess around with the screen size, version of the platform, and more to really see how the app is going to work.

If you went through the setup wizard properly on the last steps, you could already have the emulator in place on your computer. But we are going to take a moment to set up a brand new emulator in case you missed this option before or if you would like to choose a second emulator on the computer.

To get started on this is to click on the AVD Manager. You should be able to look inside of the toolbar for the icon that has the Android popping up and is beside a device with a purple display. The Android Studio is going to have one of these setups that you are able to use, and you will be able to see some details about the type of the emulator, the API that it uses, and the CPU instructions.

But if you would like to create a brand new AVD, you will just need to click on the Create Virtual Device. Now you will need to come up with some choices. For the first one, you will need to decide which device you would like to emulate. You should be able to look over to the left and see a list of categories that basically list all of the devices that you will be able to emulate and then you can see the different devices in each category. To make things simple, we are going to click on the Phone category and choose the Nexus S. once you pick this one, click on the Next.

Now you also need to decide on the Android version you would like to use. There are a few options that are available, and we are going to pick one of them, Lollipop. Check that when you are on this that the ABI column shows a value of x86 to ensure that the emulator is going to run at a good speed. Click on the Next button. This page should basically be a confirmation screen that you should double check before clicking on Finish and ending this process.

At this point, you have created a brand new virtual device that will allow you to test out your app. You should close down the AVD Manager and then head back to your main screen of the Android Studio. For the final step, you will click on Run before another window shows up and you can choose which device you want to test this app on. You shouldn't have any of the devices running here so you can start with the AVD that you created earlier, just make sure to click on the Launch Emulator and that the AVD is selected before clicking on OK.

Here you will need to give the emulator some time to load up, and you may even need to do this a few times to get it right. Once all of this is loaded properly, you will be able to see what there is of the running app.

So now that this emulator is all set up, it is time to add a bit more to the code that we did earlier so that we can see how it is going to work on other Android devices. We are going to keep this one simple right now, but you can always expand on this to get more out of it. So to start on this, you will need to go to res/values/strings.xml and then double click on this file. We are going to change this so that we can make it a bit more personal and have some fun with it. Here is the syntax of what you should type in:

<string name = "hello_world">I am learning Android!

</string>

You would be able to change up the code to say anything that you would like inside of this part of the code, making the string a lot longer, changing up the message, and so much more. This is just a great little way of showing how the code can work. But with this one, you have created your first app and even made some changes to make it a bit more personalized. You will just need to click on Run when it is done, and the message that you wrote out should show up on the screen.

Chapter 5: Doing Updates with the SDK Manager

Now we are going to take some time to do a bit more with the app that you want to create. This is all going to work regardless of the version of SDK that you would download on your computer so even if one of the older versions is there; it will still work. If you would like to make sure to open up the SDK Manager from inside the project, you will just need to click on the button that has the downward arrow with your Android peeking above it. When we are done with this section, we are going to be able to make a lot of changes to the app, and we will have one that has a PNG image, has an editable text field, and so much more.

So at this point, we need to have our "Hello, World!" app open and ready to go on the device, or you can use the emulator if that is the method that you would like to work with so that the message is showing. But now it is time to take this over to the next level.

Getting started on this project

For this one, we are going to take a moment to look ahead. The first thing that you will want to do with this step of the project is to make sure that the app is going to be simple. You don't want to add in a lot of complexities at this part because this can slow down the app, introduces some more bugs to the system, and just makes it more difficult for the user to work with. You only want to add in extra parts if you really need it for the app to work properly, but right now this is going to take some more time and work than what we want to work with at the time.

So to get started, we are going to need to open up the app/res/layout/activity_main.xml. If you are able to see the .raw and .xml file, you will be good to go. But if this is not showing up, you will need to go to the bottom of your screen and see if you need to switch all of this over to the Text mode. All we will do at this point is work to get rid of some of the attributes that are just padding to it. The Studio often adds these things to the .xml file on its own, but it can make it harder to work on the file. You are going to want to look for and delete all of these lines before we continue:

android:paddingLeft="@dimen/activity_horizontal_margin

android:paddingRight=@dimen/activity_horizontal_margin

android:paddingTop=@dimen/activity_vertical_margin

android:paddingBottom=@dimen/activity_vertical_margin

If you went through all of this and did it the proper way, your new .xml file is going to look like the following:

<RelativeLayout

xmlns:android=http://schemas.android.com/apk/res/android

xmlns:tools=http://schemas.android.com/tools

android:layout_width="match_parent"

android:layout_height="match_parent"

tools:context=".MainActivity">

<TextView

android:text="@string/hello_world

android:layout_width="wrap_content"

android:layout_height="wrap_content"/>

</RelativeLayout>

At this point, we will need to look for the Mainactivity.java part of the code. You will need to look on the left pane that is inside of Studio and then double click on it. We are going to take a moment to look at the very first piece of code, and you will need to move out a few of the lines including the following:

@Override

public boolean onOptionsItemSelected(MenuItem item){

```
//Handle action bar item clicks here. The action bar will

//automatically handle clicks on the Home/Up button, so long

//as you specify a parent activity in AndroidManifest.xml.

int id = item.getItemId();


//noinspection SimplifiableIfStatement

if (id == R.id.action_settings){

return true;

}


return super.onOptionsItemSelected(item);

}
```

You should be careful when you are doing this to make sure that you are leaving the final curly brace in its place when you delete the other options. This is the curly brace that is going to close up your class ahead of it, and you want to make sure that it is still there. Now that all the housekeeping work has been done, it is time to get to work and give the Activity a new life of its own.

Chapter 6: How to Publish Your Android App

Now that we have had some time to create our own app a little bit and learn how to manage the app in a way that makes it have less stuff in the way and so that it does more of the work that you want, it is time to learn how to publish your own app. You are going to work with making a lot of different types of apps over the years when you get familiar with working with the Android operating system and it is likely that you will at some point want to be able to publish one of the apps to make some money or for other people to be able to use it as well. In this chapter, we are going to spend some time learning how to take one of the apps that you create and getting it published.

The first thing to know is that when creating an Android app, you will need to publish it on the Google Play store. This means that you will need to create your own account using the Google Play Developer Console. This account is going to cost a little bit of money to create, about $25 at the publishing of this book, but considering the other parts of the operating system are free, this isn't so bad. The reason that there are fees with this account is that the Google company wants to keep out people who would make duplicate or fake accounts and helps to avoid people flooding the store with bad apps that no one else wants.

After you have gone through and created the account and paid the beginning fees, you are going to have your own Google Play Developer Account. You will be able to choose as many apps as you would like to publish on this account and you can choose whether you would like to publish those apps for free for others to use or in a manner to make money through the system. Some people are turned away by the fees, but if you are looking to make some money with this system on your apps by selling them, you will find that you can quickly make this $25 back. You can also allow ads to be on your app and earn some ad-revenue if you would like.

So to get this started, you just need to visit the site https://developer.android.com/distribute/index.html. Then you will just need to follow the steps that come up on the prompts to help you figure out what you are supposed to do to finish the account. In the end, you will finish creating your own developer account, pay the fees that are associated with the account to get it started, and then complete the process.

Android Crash Course: Step by Step Guide To Mastering Android Programming!

At this point, you are probably done with creating your append are ready to upload it into the system. You will just need to upload the app file in a manner that is similar to how you would attach a link or a document into your email. Then you will be asked to take a survey. This is not something that you will be able to skip out on because the system wants to know about the different factors and features about your app. Some of the questions that it is going to ask is about whether there are inappropriate contents inside and if there are any age restrictions on using the app.

After you are done with setting up your account and getting the app to upload inside of the program, you are going to need to give Google a few days in order to validate the app. You will be able to add in as many of these apps as you would like over time, but you still need to give it a few days before it is going to show up inside the app store.

And that is all that you would need to do in order to get the app to work inside of the Google Play Store. You will be able to choose to offer the game for free, add some ad revenue into the system to make money, or charge for people to use the app in the first place. There are many options about the type of apps that you are able to use, and since it is so easy to add it to the Google store, you will be able to develop the app, get it put up, and move on to the next project in no time.

Conclusion

The Android operating system is a great one for you to learn how to use whenever
you are looking to create an app or another program that works on phones,
tablets, televisions and other mobile options. It is based on the Linux system
which makes it easy to learn how to use (especially if you already know how to
use this system), and you will find that over 100 coding languages are recognized
on Android, so you are able to pick the one that is best for you.

In this guidebook, we took some time to look at the different parts of the Android
operating system. We started out with some of the basics of this system before
moving on to how set up the architecture that is inside of the code, how to create
one of your own programs, and even how to set up an emulator so that you can
run the code on your computer (which can be nice if you don't have a specific
Android device around) and see how it is going to work for you.

There is so much to love with the Android operating system. With billions of
devices around the world using this system for making apps or running the
programs that they want on their mobile devices, it is easy to learn how to use
this operating system for developing your own apps or for your own personal use.
Use this guidebook to learn more about how the Android operating system works
and to make it create the best programs for you..